FAITHFULNESS

THE FOUNDATION OF TRUE FRIENDSHIP

*6 Studies for Groups or Individuals
With Notes for Leaders*

JACALYN EYRE

Inter-Varsity Press

INTER-VARSITY PRESS
38 De Montfort Street, Leicester LE1 7GP, England

First published in the USA by Zondervan Publishing House in 1991

First British edition 1992

British Library Cataloguing in Publication Data

A catalogue record for this book is available from the British Library.

ISBN 0-85111-358-3

Typeset and printed in the United States of America

Inter-Varsity Press is the book-publishing division of the Universities and Colleges Christian Fellowship (formerly the Inter-Varsity Fellowship), a student movement linking Christian Unions in universities and colleges throughout the United Kingdom and the Republic of Ireland, and a member movement of the International Fellowship of Evangelical Students. For information about local and national activities write to UCCF, 38 De Montfort Street, Leicester LE1 7GP.

92   93   94 / DP / 5   4   3

Contents

To *our faithful friends*
during our London pilgrimage
Robert, Sue, Rachel, Alexa

Fruit of the Spirit
Bible Studies

WELCOME TO Fruit of the Spirit Bible Studies. This series was written with one goal in mind—to allow the Spirit of God to use the Word of God to produce his fruit in your life.

To get the most from this series you need to understand a few basic facts:

Fruit of the Spirit Bible Studies are designed to be flexible. You can use them in your quiet times or for group discussion. They are ideal for Sunday-school classes, small groups, or neighborhood Bible studies.

The eight guides in this series can be used in any order that is best for you or your group.

Because each guide contains only six studies, you can easily explore more than one fruit of the Spirit. In a Sunday-school class, any two guides can be combined for a quarter (twelve weeks), or the entire series can be covered in a year.

Each study deliberately focuses on only one or two passages. That allows you to see each passage in its context, avoiding the temptation of prooftexting and the frustration of "Bible hopscotch" (jumping from verse to verse). If you would like to look up additional passages, a Bible concordance will give the most help.

The questions help you *discover* what the Bible says rather than simply *telling* you what it says. They encourage you to think and to explore options rather than to merely fill in the blanks with one-word answers.

Leader's notes are provided in the back of the guide. They show how to lead a group discussion, provide additional information on questions, and suggest ways to deal with problems that may come up in the discussion. With such helps, someone with little or no experience can lead an effective study.

Suggestions for Individual Study

1. Begin each study with prayer. Ask God to help you understand the passage and to apply it to your life.

2. A good modern translation, such as the New International Version, the New American Standard Bible, or the Revised Standard Version, will give you the most help. However, the questions in this guide are based on the New International Version.

3. Read and reread the passage(s). You must know what the passage says before you can understand what it means and how it applies to you.

4. Write your answers in the space provided in the study guide. This will help you to clearly express your understanding of the passage.

5. Keep a Bible dictionary handy. Use it to look up any unfamiliar words, names, or places.

Suggestions for Group Study

1. Come to the study prepared. Careful preparation will greatly enrich your time in group discussion.

2. Be willing to join in the discussion. The leader of the group will not be lecturing but will encourage people to discuss what they have learned in the passage. Plan to share what God has taught you in your individual study.

3. Stick to the passage being studied. Base your answers on the verses being discussed rather than on outside authorities such as commentaries or your favorite author or speaker.

4. Try to be sensitive to the other members of the group. Listen attentively when they speak, and be affirming whenever you can. This will encourage more hesitant members of the group to participate.

5. Be careful not to dominate the discussion. By all means participate! But allow others to have equal time.

6. If you are the discussion leader, you will find additional suggestions and helpful ideas in the leader's notes at the back of the guide.

FAITHFULNESS
The Foundation of True Friendship

WHERE DO WE GO from here?"

Our family had just moved to England on a limited ministry assignment. Because we would only be here a year or so, we did not bring our furniture. So my husband and I and our three boys undertook our adventure with two suitcases apiece.

We were staying with colleagues while we looked for a place to live. We exhausted the ads in the newspaper. Everything seemed too small or too expensive. In a new country without familiar resources, we felt very disoriented and vulnerable.

From out of the blue, a woman stepped from the crowd at the church where we were visiting. She introduced herself as Sharon and then proceeded to ask enough questions to know everything about us.

Sharon then, much to our surprise, warmly offered her services. She helped us find a house, negotiate terms, connect the utilities, locate furniture, and she provided transportation. Two weeks after our initial meeting we were comfortably settled in the perfect house for our family.

We continued to benefit from Sharon's hospitality through our entire stay in England. There were times when we felt we asked too much and when we feared we were imposing. But we never got any such signals from our "hostess." She and her family were there to continue to welcome and receive us. The message spoken and lived was, "You can depend on us."

God values such faithful friendships. In fact, God is the source and standard of friendship. In the Old Testament, God demonstrates the meaning of faithfulness as he calls Abraham, encourages Joshua, and forgives and loves Israel.

In the New Testament, Jesus is our model of faithfulness. He is not only the Lord of the disciples but also their friend. Jesus tells them in John 15:15, "I no longer call you servants, because a servant does not know his master's business. Instead, I have called you friends."

Scripture also contains numerous examples of men and women who committed themselves to God and to each other and who became faithful friends. Joshua worked for years as a faithful friend and aid to Moses. Ruth was a faithful companion to Naomi when life seemed filled with death, failure, and hopelessness. Jonathan was the friend of David and helped him even at the cost of Saul's anger and Jonathan's own claim to the throne. Barnabus was a faithful friend to the Apostle Paul and was there to sponsor him when Paul was held in suspicion by the early church.

The faithful friendships between these people in the Scriptures brought blessings beyond measure. Joshua became the general who led Israel into the Promised Land. Ruth married into the nation of Israel and became the grandmother of king David and part of the line leading to the Messiah. Jonathan's friendship to David opened the way for David to become the great king whose ultimate heir would be Jesus Christ. And Barnabus launched Paul into a ministry that spread the gospel through the Roman Empire.

We all need faithful friends. And, just as importantly, we need to learn to *be* faithful in our friendships. As you work through this Fruit of the Spirit Bible Study, you will discover that faithfulness includes: a commitment to be there the way Ruth was for Naomi; a willingness to forgive the way Hosea forgave his adulterous wife; a promise of support the way God supported Joshua as he led Israel; an honoring of commitments the way God required of Israel in a time of social decay; and a fulfilling of responsibilities the way Jesus taught his disciples just before his crucifixion. Finally, because faithfulness is difficult, we need to know that there are rewards for those who make the determined effort.

May God cause the fruit of faithfulness to grow in all of your relationships.

1

A Commitment to Be There

THERE IS AN OLD SAYING that when times are hardest you know who your friends are. That summarizes the first chapter of the book of Ruth.

Naomi's situation was at its worst. She had lost her husband and sons, which meant that she also lost her source of income, security, and identity. She was without hope. It is at this point that Ruth, her daughter-in-law, does an astonishing thing—she decides to stay with Naomi. Ruth demonstrates a commitment to be there.

1. Why is faithfulness an important quality in friendship?

2. Read Ruth 1. What do we learn about Naomi in verses 1–5?

3. Ruth and Orpah are introduced as Naomi's daughters-in-law (v. 4). What basis do these three women have for mutual trust (vv. 1–5)?

4. Consider a time when you shared a difficult experience with someone. How did it strengthen your friendship?

5. What do verses 6–13 reveal about Naomi's relationship to God?

6. When you have faced a painful experience, how has it affected your attitude toward God?

7. The famine is over, and Naomi prepares to return to Bethlehem with her daughters-in-law. Why does Naomi encourage Ruth and Orpah to stay in Moab (vv. 8–14)?

8. What cost does Naomi face by encouraging Ruth and Orpah to stay in Moab?

How do both Ruth and Orpah show faithfulness to Naomi by their different responses?

9. What does it cost you to be faithful to those you love?

10. Read Ruth's familiar words in verses 16–17. How would you summarize her words of dedication?

11. Naomi's homecoming is painful (vv. 19–22). How does Naomi view herself and her situation?

12. What provisions has God made for Naomi even in the midst of this bitter time?

13. In what situations is it most important for us to "be there" for our loved ones and friends?

How does Ruth's example encourage you to be faithful in good times and in bad?

2

A Willingness to Forgive

SHALLOW RELATIONSHIPS CHARACTERIZE our culture. Job transfers from city to city expand our contacts but keep our roots shallow. It is easy just to think about finding new friends when we run into problems with our current ones.

God isn't like that. As we see from the book of Hosea, God makes commitments for both time and eternity. Through the faithful prophet Hosea, who reclaims his adulterous wife, God shows what lengths he is willing to go to in forgiving and being faithful to us.

1. Why do you think forgiveness is one of the foundations of friendship?

2. Read Hosea 2:19–3:5. Looking back at 2:13, how would you describe the spiritual condition of Israel?

3. The word *betroth* is used three times in verses 19–20. What virtues and qualities characterize this commitment?

4. God describes Israel's restoration in terms of marriage because he views idolatry as spiritual adultery. Why do you think God uses such a graphic term?

5. In what areas are God's people in our time and culture tempted to be unfaithful to God?

In what areas do you struggle to be faithful to God?

6. The destroyed relationship between God and Israel is repaired because God is willing to forgive. How would you describe the overflowing benefits that come from this reconciled relationship (vv. 21–23)?

7. Why can it be so difficult to forgive those who are close to us?

What overflowing benefits result when we do forgive?

8. God tells Hosea to reclaim his unfaithful wife (3:1–5). What roles do Hosea and Gomer play in this reconciliation (2:19–3:5)?

9. Hosea must pay a price to reclaim Gomer (v.2). How does Hosea's restoration of Gomer foreshadow the ministry of Jesus Christ?

10. Forgiving love is costly. What price have you paid when forgiving another?

   How does this passage motivate you to do whatever is necessary to forgive?

11. How does this passage encourage you in your relationship to God?

3

A Promise of Support

AT OUR CHURCH WE SING the words "Be bold, be strong, for the Lord your God is with you." My youngest son thought we were singing "Be bald, be strong . . ."

As Joshua faced the daunting task of following Moses, I can imagine that he felt exposed and bald.

At times we all accept responsibilities that seem overwhelming. How well we perform frequently depends on the support and friendship of those around us.

In this chapter Joshua moves into a new "pastoral position" of leading over a million people. As the Lord promises to support Joshua, we observe a new facet of faithfulness and friendship.

1. Recall a time when you took on a project or responsibility that seemed too massive. How did you feel?

2. Read Joshua 1:1–9. Moses is dead. How do you think Joshua would have felt about becoming Israel's leader after forty years of Moses' leadership?

3. As Joshua begins to lead Israel into the Promised Land, what assurances does God give him (vv. 1–5)?

4. God promises to be with Joshua (v. 5). Why would that be encouraging?

5. What difference does it make when someone offers to come with you to accomplish a hard task?

6. What does God require of Joshua in order to be successful and prosperous in leading Israel (vv. 6–9)?

7. Joshua must meditate on the Law day and night (v. 8). How do you think this would help him to lead Israel?

8. How have you been supported and strengthend by a knowledge of the Scriptures?

9. How can we use Scripture to comfort and strengthen those who need our support?

10. God tells Joshua not to be discouraged or terrified (v. 9). Why do you think this command was necessary?

11. How can God's command to be bold in the face of hard circumstances give us strength?

12. Throughout this passage, how is the Lord himself a model of what it means to be a supportive friend?

13. Think of a friend who needs your support during difficult times. How can you follow the Lord's example in helping that person?

4

Honoring Our Commitments

I PROMISED A FRIEND that I would care for her three children tonight while she attends a class. I would much prefer to spend the evening with a good book. I have had a very busy day, I am just getting over the flu, and dinner is waiting to be fixed.

Commitments are not always convenient. But God expects us to keep them. When we do, we benefit, others benefit, and God is pleased. In this study we look at a time in Israel when past commitments were not taken seriously and so were disregarded. In turn, Israel feared that God had abandoned his commitment to them. God speaks into this time of cynicism and unbelief to call Israel back the covenant.

1. Think of a time when someone broke a commitment to you. How did it make you feel?

2. Read Malachi 2:10–16. These verses are full of broken commitments. What specific commitments have been broken?

3. Consider the three questions posed in verse 10. What point is Malachi trying to make?

4. Many churches struggle with internal conflicts. How could Malachi's questions help?

5. What is God's attitude toward Israel's marrying "the daughter of a foreign God" (v. 11)?

6. Intermarriage with pagans was strictly forbidden because it could lead to apostasy (see Ex. 34:15–16; Deut. 7:3–4). How does this explain Malachi's seemingly harsh prayer in verse 12?

7. We are influenced by the people with whom we are closest (spouses, friends, business partners, and so on). What can we learn from verses 11 and 12?

8. The people are confused as to why God does not accept them (v. 13). What is the problem (vv. 14–16)?

9. By observing key words or phrases like *broken faith*, *partner*, and *marriage covenant* (vv. 14–15), what can we learn about God's view of marriage?

10. How does God's view of marriage help us understand his attitude toward divorce (v. 16)?

11. How can knowing God's view of marriage enrich our own marriages? our friendships?

12. Healthy relationships require that we "do not break faith" with those to whom we have committed ourselves (vv. 15–16). How can honoring our commitments make a difference in the way we relate to our spouse or our friends?

13. Think of commitments you have made to family or friends. Which ones have you been careless about keeping?

What can you do to better honor those commitments?

5

Fulfilling Our Responsibilities

FRIENDSHIP WITH OTHERS begins with our friendship with God. "You are my friends if you do what I command" (John 15:14). In all relationships there are commitments and obligations. This is especially true in our relationship with God.

In the parable of the talents, Jesus describes his expectations and requirements of his disciples. He calls us to make investments for him, to choose his goals, and then ultimately to "come and share" his happiness. We are called into a relationship of responsibility and friendship.

1. What types of responsibility do you enjoy?

What types of responsibility do you avoid?

2. Read Matthew 25:14–30. As the master leaves on a long journey, what resources does he give each of his servants (vv. 14–15)?

What does he expect of his servants?

3. What are some of the resources Jesus has given to you?

What do you think Jesus expects of you?

4. How does the master show approval to the servants who please him (vv. 21, 23)

5. Recall a time when you sensed God's approval. What was it like?

6. How would you describe the behavior of the wicked servant (vv. 24–30)?

Why do you think the third servant did not invest his master's money?

7. What image does the third servant have of his master (vv. 24–25)?

How does our image of Jesus affect the way we serve him?

8. How does the master show his disapproval (vv. 26–30)?

9. The third servant receives a harsh judgment (vv. 28–30). What does Jesus want us to understand about our responsibilities within his kingdom?

10. What investments can you make for the sake of God's kingdom?

11. From this passage, what can we learn about our relationship with God?

How can these principles be applied to our other friendships?

Let love and faithfulness never leave you; bind them around your neck, write them on the tablet of your heart. Then you will win favor and a good name in the sight of God and man.

Proverbs 3:3−4

Through love and faithfulness sin is atoned for; through the fear of the Lord a man avoids evil.

Proverbs 16:6

Love and faithfulness keep a king safe; through love his throne is made secure.

Proverbs 20:28

Like a bad tooth or a lame foot is reliance on the unfaithful in times of trouble.

Proverbs 25:19

6

The Rewards of Faithfulness

V ERY EARLY WE DISCOVERED THAT our son Jeremy was motivated by rewards. A five-hour task could be reduced to five minutes if an appropriate reward was offered.

Faithfulness is a life-long task that requires continual effort. In these proverbs God shows us that there are rich rewards for those who do the hard work.

---

1. What benefits are there in being faithful to a friend?

---

2. Read the four Proverbs on page 32. What are some of the benefits of faithfulness?

3. Faithfulness is paired with love in three of the four references. How are the two words complementary?

4. Look at Proverbs 3:3–4. What efforts does it take to gain and keep a good reputation?

5. What are some of the benefits of a good reputation?

   What are the liabilities of a poor reputation?

6. Look at Proverbs 16:6. Faithfulness can help us overcome past sins against God and others. How do you think this works in practice?

7. Fear of the Lord is parallel with faithfulness in this proverb. How are faithfulness and fear of the Lord complementary truths?

8. How can faithfulness help us to live a godly life?

9. Look at Proverbs 20:28. Love and faithfulness aren't traditionally hot topics on the political circuit. How would they contribute to a healthy government?

10. How would it affect your attitude toward government to know that your political leaders were seeking to act in love and faithfulness?

11. Look at Proverbs 25:19. How do a bad tooth and a lame foot describe what it is like to depend on an unfaithful person?

12. We have all had the experience of being let down by someone. How are you affected?

    How do you tend to respond?

13. A life full of faithfulness is a rich life. How do the practical benefits of faithfulness motivate you to be a more faithful person to God and to your friends?

Leader's Notes

LEADING A BIBLE DISCUSSION—especially for the first time—can make you feel both nervous and excited. If you are nervous, realize that you are in good company. Many biblical leaders, such as Moses, Joshua, and the apostle Paul, felt nervous and inadequate to lead others (see, for example, 1 Cor. 2:3). Yet God's grace was sufficient for them, just as it will be for you.

Some excitement is also natural. Your leadership is a gift to the others in the group. Keep in mind, however, that other group members also share responsibility for the group. Your role is simply to stimulate discussion by asking questions and encouraging people to respond. The suggestions listed below can help you to be an effective leader.

Preparing to Lead

1. Ask God to help you understand and apply the passage to your own life. Unless that happens, you will not be prepared to lead others.

2. Carefully work through each question in the study guide. Meditate and reflect on the passage as you formulate your answers.

3. Familiarize yourself with the leader's notes for the study. These will help you understand the purpose of the study and will provide valuable information about the questions in the study.

4. Pray for the various members of the group. Ask God to use these studies to bring about greater spiritual fruit in the life of each person.

5. Before the first meeting, make sure each person has a study guide. Encourage them to prepare beforehand for each study.

Leading the Study

1. Begin the study on time. If people realize that the study begins on schedule, they will work harder to arrive on time.

2. At the beginning of your first time together, explain that these studies are designed to be discussions not lectures. Encourage everyone to participate, but realize that some may be hesitant to speak during the first few sessions.

3. Read the introductory paragraph at the beginning of the discussion. This will orient the group to the passage being studied.

4. Read the passage aloud. You may choose to do this yourself, or you might ask for volunteers.

5. The questions in the guide are designed to be used just as they are written. If you wish, you may simply read each one aloud to the group. Or you may prefer to express them in your own words. However, unnecessary rewording of the questions is not recommended.

6. Don't be afraid of silence. People in the group may need time to think before responding.

7. Avoid answering your own questions. If necessary, rephrase a question until it is clearly understood. Even an eager group will quickly become passive and silent if they think the leader will do most of the talking.

8. Encourage more than one answer to each question. Ask, "What do the rest of you think?" or "Anyone else?" until several people have had a chance to respond.

9. Try to be affirming whenever possible. Let people know you appreciate their insights into the passage.

10. Never reject an answer. If it is clearly wrong, ask, "Which verse led you to that conclusion?" Or let the group handle the problem by asking them what they think about the question.

11. Avoid going off on tangents. If people wander off course, gently bring them back to the passage being considered.

12. Conclude your time together with conversational prayer. Ask God to help you apply those things that you learned in the study.

13. End on time. This will be easier if you control the pace of the discussion by not spending too much time on some questions or too little on others.

Many more suggestions and helps are found in the book *Leading Bible Discussions* (InterVarsity Press). Reading that would be well worth your time.

STUDY 1
A *Commitment to Be There*
Ruth 1

Purpose: To discover that faithfulness requires that we stay with a person not only in good times but also in adversity.

The book of Ruth shows us ordinary people who trust in the providence of God as they face painful events in life. The setting is in the days of the Judges, when the faith of Israel is at a low point. The book reflects a time in which there is social unrest, violence, asocial disintegration, sexual immorality, and war.

Question 1. Every study begins with an "approach question," which is discussed *before* reading the passage. An approach question is designed to do three things.

First, it helps to break the ice. Because an approach question doesn't require any knowledge of the passage or any special preparation, it can get people talking and can help them to warm up to each other.

Second, an approach question can motivate people to study the passage at hand. At the beginning of the study, people in the group aren't necessarily ready to jump into the world of the Bible. Their minds may be on other things (their kids, a problem at work, an upcoming meeting) that have nothing to do with the study. An approach question can capture their interest and draw them into the discussion by raising important issues related to the study. The question becomes a bridge between their personal lives and the answers found in Scripture.

Third, a good approach question can reveal where people's thoughts or feelings need to be transformed by Scripture. That is why it is important to ask the approach question *before* reading the passage. The passage might inhibit the spontaneous, honest answers people might have given, because they feel compelled to give biblical answers. The approach question allows them to compare their personal thoughts and feelings with what they later discover in Scripture.

Question 2. Naomi was left abandoned and hopeless with the death of her husband and sons. In the Old Testament a Hebrew woman was her husband's possession. Although she was more than a slave, she had very few rights, and no inheritance rights. Any position of respect in the community grew out of the male children she bore.

The word translated as "widow" communicates loneliness, abandonment, and helplessness. The only hope of recovery of social status for a widow was to marry a second time.

Question 5. Naomi is honest with her feelings. She does not hide her pain, anger, hurt, or belief that God "has gone out against me." She also does not hide her affection and concern for her daughters-in-law.

Question 7. Naomi encouraged Ruth and Oprah to stay in Moab because of her love for them. It would have been easier to keep them by her side. She faced the hard experience of being an outcast in her own country as she was returning without a husband or sons. Naomi didn't want her daughters-in-law to experience life as foreigners in Israel. While God had made provisions for aliens in the law, they were not particularly welcome and were usually excluded from the life of the community.

Question 8. Orpah shows her love to Naomi by being obedient to Naomi's wish. Ruth shows her love by remaining with Naomi. The word *clung* (1:14) is a verb meaning a committed, faithful "cleaving" in a deep personal relationship.

Background material for this study comes from David Atkinson,

The Message of Ruth, The Bible Speaks Today (Downers Grove, Ill.: InterVarsity Press).

STUDY 2
A Willingness to Forgive
Hosea 2:19—3:5

Purpose: To consider how faithfulness seeks forgiveness and reconciliation by looking at God's forgiveness of Israel in the book of Hosea.

The behavior of Gomer is not an indictment of the women of Israel, but of the nation of Israel. All of Israel worshiped the Baals and were therefore guilty of physical and spiritual adultery.

As you study the book of Hosea, it is important to keep in mind that forgiveness is not a given, but is God's free choice. When God grants forgiveness, it is an astounding act of grace.

Question 2. The events in Hosea took place during the reign of Jeroboam II, king of Israel. It was a prosperous time, and Hosea's prophecy of coming judgment must have seemed farfetched. Israel adopted a Canaanite lifestyle which included worship of their gods. The Baals of the Canaanites were regarded as a source of fertility and prosperity. Orgiastic worship at the shrines was the centerpiece of their religion. In essence, such religion was the opposite of everything embodied in God's covenant.

Question 3. Verses 19—20 focus on the legal and contractual nature of the new relationship. In Israelite marriages a betrothal would involve negotiations with the bride's family for a proper bride price, which the suitor would pay. A period of time would pass between the betrothal and the consummation of the relationship, but in that interval the woman was considered to belong officially to her intended and to belong to him for life. The intensity of God's betrothal to Israel is conveyed by repeating the word *betroth* three times (David Allan Hubbard, *Hosea*, The Tyndale Old Testament Commentaries [Downers Grove, Ill.: InterVarsity Press, 1989].

Question 4. The worship of the Baals actually involved sexual acts. But beyond that, the relationship between God and his people was one of deep personal intimacy. In the covenant God gave himself to his people and expected no less in return.

Questions 6–7. The benefits of forgiveness are more than personal. Verses 21–23 show that the skies (rain) and the earth (crops) become fruitful and productive as God forgives and restores. Likewise, when reconciliation takes place between two people today, the benefits are more than personal. Those around us benefit as well. Encourage group members to think of how this works out in their situations. There can be benefits in attitudes, atmosphere, and even physical health.

Questions 8–9. Gomer's sexual promiscuity had evidently settled on one person. Her betrothal price was given to rescue her from financial obligations that bound her to her lover. It is possible that she was "owned" by her lover and was a slave/harlot for him. In contrast, Hosea's love was not one of ownership and slavery, but of grace and true freedom.

The real cost of restoring Israel (and the church) was paid in the sacrifice of Jesus Christ. In him, once and for all, the betrothal price and cost of redemption from our slavery to sin and Satan was paid in full.

STUDY 3
A *Promise of Support*
Joshua 1:1–9

Purpose: To realize that personal support is an important facet of faithfulness.

Question 2. Moses had an astounding relationship with God that shaped the nation forever after. His closeness to God was glimpsed when he met God face to face on the mountain top and received the Ten Commandments.

Under his leadership there were numerous miracles, such as

parting the Red Sea, water gushing from a rock, and manna and quail for food. And there were the judgments by God: destroying the golden calf, snake bites, restrictions on entering the land, and so on.

Moses' accomplishments included writing the Pentateuch and administering the Law by organizing judges of tens, hundreds, and thousands. He also set up religious worship, including the tabernacle and the Levitical priesthood.

But remember that Joshua was Moses' assistant. He saw Moses during his ordinary times. Joshua observed Moses' weaknesses, his stuttering, his temper, his disobedience, and his discouragements, as well as his great moments.

Question 3. Observe that God not only promises his presence (a promise not to be taken lightly) but also assures Joshua that there will be no successful resistance to him as long as he lives. The fact that this was the land promised to Moses and Israel's forefathers would also have been an encouragement. The land God would lead Israel into had been identified, chosen, and set aside.

Question 6. Things that God requires of Joshua include the following: strength, courage, obedience to all the law, and meditation on the law day and night.

Question 7. Meditating on the law would keep Joshua's focus on God as he took on the task of establishing the nation in the Promised Land.

STUDY 4
Honoring Our Commitments
Malachi 2:10–16

Purpose: To learn how important it is to remain faithful to God in our commitments.

Background: Malachi was written in a "silent" time. The Jews returned from their Babylonian exile with high hopes. They rebuilt the temple and the walls of Jerusalem. As the years passed, however, they became disillusioned as the expected prosperity of their country did not come. They were surrounded by enemies, and they suffered drought, bad crops, and famine. They began to doubt God's love. They saw their enemies as being blessed and began to think that there was no profit in obedience. They became cynical, unbelieving, and gave up obedience to the law (See *The New Bible Commentary: Revised* [Grand Rapids, Mich.: Eerdmans, 1970] or Joyce G. Baldwin, *Haggai, Zechariah, Malachi*, Tyndale Old Testament Commentaries [Downers Grove, Ill.: InterVarsity Press, 1972].

This is a study of commitments or, more accurately, the breaking of commitments, particularly in the area of marriage and divorce. Be sensitive as you lead the study. It is not intended to create a border of guilt. The study does, however, look at God's standards for marriage, and not all of us have been able to live up to them. (All of us have failed to live up to them inwardly.) It is important to remember that the questions and concerns raised in the study should drive us to God and his mercy rather than into despair.

Question 3. Israel is bound together by a common God, with common ancestors, and the covenant given at Mount Sinai. Malachi sees these things as the foundation of their national existence. They should bind Israel together in a community of justice and faithfulness. Malachi considers it intolerable that this unity is being broken by their sin.

The word *Father* is ambiguous. The NIV, by capitalizing the word seems to imply that it refers to God. It is more probably that it refers to one of the patriarchs, as there is no precedent in the Old Testament for referring to God as Father in the manner that Jesus taught Christians to do. The word *father* probably refers to Jacob, since Malachi refers to Jacob in 1:2; 2:12; and 3:6.

Question 6. The phrase "to be cut off from the tents of Jacob" implies that the offender is excluded from the community of Israel. The offender's sacrifice to the Lord is unacceptable because by act of intermarriage he has chosen disobedience as a way of life.

The Lord's objection to intermarriage is religious, not racial.

Question 9. Malachi emphasizes marriage as a partnership. The Hebrew word *partnership* is often used in the masculine to refer to a close friend with whom one shares interests, whether good or bad. In this text it refers to the wife.

Israelites saw marriage as a covenant to which the Lord was a witness. This should have contributed to the couple's stability and loyalty as partners.

The Hebrew underlying verse 15 is not clear. Therefore each translation contains an interpretation. The general understanding is that because of the unity between husband and wife, the rearing of children is a shared responsibility. In an atmosphere of love and stability, children can be nurtured by godly principles. Family relationships are to illustrate love and loyalty and should embody the divine covenant between God and Israel.

Question 10. Be sensitive here. There are probably people in your study who have gone through a divorce. (Perhaps even you have.) We shouldn't avoid looking at God's standards, because grace and forgiveness are available to those who come to him.

The phrase "I hate a man's covering himself with violence as well as with his garment" (v. 16) is a figurative expression that means "I hate all kinds of gross injustice" (see Joyce G. Baldwin, *Haggai, Zechariah, Malachi*).

STUDY 5
Fulfilling Our Responsibilities
Matthew 25:14—30

Purpose. To consider the importance of faithfully fulfilling our responsibilities until Jesus returns.

Question 2. The word *talent* means money. The master's expectation was that the servants would increase his wealth.

Question 3. Many often see the "talents" in this passage as living up to our full potential. This is incorrect. The talents should not be seen as natural endowments given to people in general, but as specific privileges and opportunities of the kingdom of heaven.

It is worth considering gifts of the Spirit as well as fruits of the Spirit (love, peace, joy, faithfulness, and so on) as some of the resources that Jesus has given to us to invest.

Question 5. This is a subjective question, but it's worth the risk. God does affirm us, but unless we pay attention we can miss it. How important it is for us to know that we are pleasing to our God.

Question 6. In your discussion keep in mind Jesus' diagnosis of the servant. The servant's lack of action was a breach of trust. He represents a discipleship of playing it safe and achieving nothing. He is more concerned about not doing anything wrong than about pleasing his master. Being faithful involves active, responsible service that produces results.

Question 7. The image the servant had of his master was inaccurate. He shows what we all can do—create wrong images of God to justify sinful behavior.

The master answers him in such a way as to show how distorted the wicked servant's thinking was. If in fact the master was so harsh, then the wicked servant should have been very careful to make investments with the money given him.

Question 9. Failure to be responsible with the investments of the kingdom carries with it the penalty of having those investments withdrawn. When they are withdrawn, we have nothing that entitles us to enter into the joy of the Lord. Our happiness is denied. The servant becomes useless and destined to stay in darkness.

Resources for the Gospel of Matthew include Richard France, *Matthew*, Tyndale New Testament Commentaries (Grand Rapids, Mich.: Eerdmans, 1987) and R. V. G. Tasker, *The Gospel of Matthew*, Tyndale New Testament Commentaries (Grand Rapids, Mich.: Eerdmans, 1961).

STUDY 6
The Rewards of Faithfulness
Proverbs 3:3—4; 16:6; 20:28; 25:19

Purpose: To encourage people to pursue a life of faithfulness by learning that the faithful are rewarded and that unfaithful people cannot be trusted.

Faithfulness in the Old Testament involved keeping the covenant between God and his people. God promised to take Israel as his people and to be their God. In return, Israel promised to worship God and to keep his law.

The word *faithful* can also be translated as "true." The central idea is that one who is faithful and conforms to the standard of God's law is therefore straight and true, not crooked, bent, or falling short.

Question 3. The key to interpreting a proverb is to pay attention to the parallel words and phrases. The two words or phrases often carry the same idea but from a different angle. By comparing the two, their meaning is enriched and deepened.

Question 4. A life characterized by faithfulness does not come easily; it requires determination. We must choose to be faithful every day and in each situation.

Question 6. Of course only the death of Jesus Christ can atone for sin. But this proverb is not meant to be a theological statement. Practically speaking, if we are faithful and loving toward those we have hurt and offended, it is possible that we can make restitution. God is pleased with us when we seek to act in love and faithfulness even though we have failed to do so in the past.

Questions 7—8. Fear of the Lord is a parallel of faithfulness. Faithfulness to God enables us to be faithful in the rest of our lives.

Questions 9—10. Any political system will fail if it is not built on moral values. Corrupt governments destroy their own foundations and create oppression, resentment and, ultimately, rebellion. On the other hand, governments that show faithfulness and love create a climate of trust and goodwill that results in stability.